# Presenting
# Exchange Server 2016
# & Exchange Online

**IT Pro Solutions**

**William R. Stanek**

Author & Series Editor

# Presenting Exchange Server 2016 & Exchange Online

Stanek & Associates publishes in a variety of formats, including print, electronic and by print-on-demand. Some materials included with standard print editions may not be included in electronic or print-on-demand editions or vice versa.

**Country of First Publication**: United States of America.

**Cover Design**: Creative Designs Ltd.
**Editorial Development**: Andover Publishing Solutions
**Technical Review**: L & L Technical Content Services

You can provide feedback related to this book by emailing the author at williamstanek@aol.com. Please use the name of the book as the subject line.

Version: 1.0.0.5a

> **Note** I may periodically update this text and the version number shown above will let you know which version you are working with. If there's a specific feature you'd like me to write about in an update, message me on Facebook (http://facebook.com/williamstanekauthor). Please keep in mind readership of this book determines how much time I can dedicate to it.

Thank you for purchasing *Presenting Exchange*! I hope you find this book useful and helpful as you set out to work with Exchange Server 2016 and Exchange Online.

# Table of Contents

# 1. Introducing Exchange 2016

Before getting to the specifics of working with Exchange 2016, take a few moments to familiarize yourself with the configuration options available. Microsoft Exchange is available in on-premises, online and hybrid implementations.

With an on-premises implementation, you deploy Exchange server hardware on your network and manage all aspects of the implementation. Here, you control the servers and determine which version of Exchange those servers will run. Exchange Server 2016 is the current version of Exchange, and was released in its original implementation in October 2015. Like other releases of Exchange, Exchange Server 2016 is updated periodically with software updates which may change or enhance the options available.

With an online implementation, you manage the service-level settings, organization configuration, and recipient configuration while relying on Microsoft for hardware and other services. Microsoft determines which version of Exchange those servers will run. Online implementations always use the most current release version of Exchange, which at present is Exchange Server 2016. As with any on-premises implementation, Microsoft's servers are updated periodically with software updates which may change or enhance the options available.

Although either an on-premises or online implementation can be your only solution for all your enterprise messaging needs, a hybrid implementation gives you an integrated online and on-premises solution. Here, your organization controls the on-premises servers and Microsoft controls the online servers. The on-premises servers and online servers can run the same, or different, versions of Exchange.

Understanding the various implementation scenarios will help you work through the rest of this book and will also help you navigate Exchange 2016 and its management options on your own. This chapter covers the basics. You'll learn about Exchange Admin Center and Exchange Management Shell, the essential tools for managing Exchange 2016.

As you get started with Exchange 2016, it's important to point out that with this version, Microsoft has completed the consolidation of server roles begun with Exchange 2013. Thus, Mailbox and Edge Transport are now the only server roles available. Mailbox servers now perform all messaging and client access tasks except for perimeter security, which can be handled by servers running the Edge Transport role.

# 2. Getting Started with Exchange Admin Center

Exchange Admin Center replaces Exchange Management Console and Exchange Control Panel (ECP) used in early releases of Exchange and there is no longer a separate graphical administration tool. Exchange Admin Center is a browser-based application designed for managing on-premises, online, and hybrid Exchange organizations.

For on-premises management, you access Exchange Admin Center through the Mailbox servers deployed in your Exchange organization. For online management, you access Exchange Admin Center through the Mailboxes servers hosted by Microsoft. Although the application can be configured with an internal access URL and a separate external access URL, only an internal access URL is configured by default in on-premises configurations. This means that by default you can access Exchange Admin Center only when you are on the corporate network.

## Navigating Exchange Admin Center Options

After you log in to Exchange Admin Center, you'll see the list view with manageable features listed in the left pane, also called the Features pane (see Figure 1). When you select a feature in the Features pane, you'll then see the related topics or "tabs" for that feature. The manageable items for a selected topic or tab are displayed in the main area of the browser window. For example, when you select Recipients in the Features pane, the topics or tabs that you can work with are:

Mailboxes, Groups, Resources, Contacts, Shared and Migration.

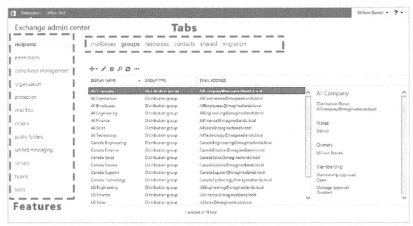

**FIGURE 1** Exchange Admin Center features and tabs

As shown in Figure 2, the navigation bar at the top of the window has several important options. You use the Enterprise and Office 365 options for cross-premises navigation. If there are notifications, you'll see a Notification icon on the Navigation bar. Clicking this icon displays notifications, such as alerts regarding automated or batch processes. The User button shows the currently logged on user. Clicking the User button allows you to logout or sign in as another user.

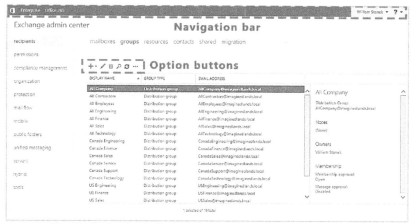

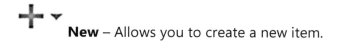

FIGURE 2  The Navigation bar in Exchange Admin Center

Below the tabs, you'll find a row of Option buttons:

**New** – Allows you to create a new item.

**Edit** – Allows you to edit a selected item.

**Delete** – Deletes a selected item.

**Search** – Performs a search within the current context.

**Refresh** – Refreshes the display so you can see changes.

**More** – If available, displays additional options.

When working with recipients, such as mailboxes or groups, you can click the More button to display options to:

- Add or remove columns
- Export data for the listed recipients to a .csv file
- Perform advanced searches

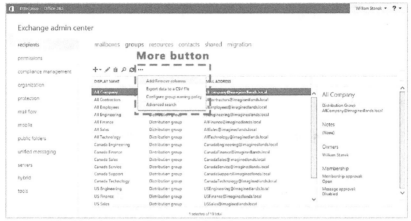

**FIGURE 3** The More button in Exchange Admin Center

If you customize the view by adding or removing columns, the settings are saved for the computer that you are using to access Exchange Admin Center. However, because the settings are saved as browser cookies, clearing the browser history will remove the custom settings.

When working with recipients, you typically can select multiple items and perform bulk editing as long as you select like items, such as mailbox users or mail-enabled contacts. Select multiple items using the Shift or Ctrl key and then use bulk editing options in the Details pane to bulk edit the selected items.

> **NOTE**   Although ECP for Exchange 2010 would return only 500 recipients at a time, Exchange Admin Center

for Exchange 2016 doesn't have this limitation. Results are paged so that you can go through results one page at a time and up to 20,000 recipients can be returned in the result set.

## Accessing Exchange Admin Center

Exchange Admin Center is designed to be used with Windows, Windows Server and other operating systems. When you are working with Windows or Windows Server, you can use Internet Explorer or the Edge browser. With other operating systems, such as Linux, you can use Firefox or Chrome. On Mac OS X 10.5 or later, you can also use Safari.

You access Exchange Admin Center by following these steps:

1. Open your web browser and enter the secure URL for Exchange Admin Center. If you are outside the corporate network, enter the external URL, such as *https://mail.imaginedlands.com/ecp*. If you are inside the corporate network, enter the internal URL, such as https://mailserver23/ecp.

2. If your browser displays a security alert stating there's a problem with the site's security certificate or that the connection is untrusted, proceed anyway. This alert is displayed because the browser does not trust the self-signed certificate that was automatically created when the Exchange server was installed.

- With Internet Explorer, the error typically states "There's a problem with this website's security certificate." Proceed by selecting the Continue To This Web Site (Not Recommended) link.
- With Google Chrome, the error typically states "The site's security certificate is not trusted." Continue by clicking Proceed Anyway.

- With Mozilla Firefox, the error typically states "This connection is untrusted." Proceed by selecting I Understand The Risks and then selecting Add Exception. Finally, in the Add Security Exception dialog box, select Confirm Security Exception.

3. You'll see the logon page for Exchange Admin Center (see Figure 4). Enter your user name and password, and then click **Sign In**.

Be sure to specify your user name in DOMAIN\username format. The domain can either be the DNS domain, such as imaginedlands.com, or the NetBIOS domain name, such as pocket-consulta. For example, the user AnneW could specify her logon name as imaginedlands.com\annew or pocket-consulta\annew.

4. If you are logging on for the first time, select your preferred display language and time zone, and then click **Save**.

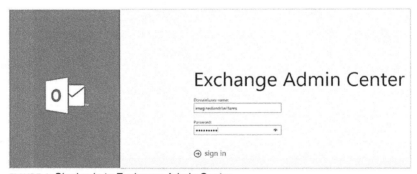

**FIGURE 4** Signing in to Exchange Admin Center

**FIGURE 5** Setting the language and time zone.

To ensure all features are available you should only use Exchange Admin Center with the most recent version of the browser available for your operating system. The version of Exchange Admin Center you see depends on the version of Exchange running on the Mailbox server hosting your personal mailbox. Exchange 2016 runs version 15.1, and you can specify this version explicitly by appending **?ExchClientVer=15** to the internal or external URL. By default, you must use HTTPS to connect. Using HTTPS ensures data transmitted between the client browser and the server is encrypted and secured.

## Authenticating and Proxying Connections

When you access Exchange Admin Center in a browser, a lot is happening in the background that you don't see. Although you access the application using a specific server in your organization, the Client Access service running on the server acts as a front-end proxy that authenticates and proxies the connection to the Exchange back end using Internet Information Services (IIS). Thus, although Mailbox server functions perform the actual back-end processing, the front-end IIS configuration is essential to proper operations.

As shown in Figure 6, you can examine the configuration settings for Exchange Admin Center and other applications using Internet Information Services (IIS) Manager. The server to which you connect processes your remote actions via the ECP application running on the default website. The physical directory for this application is %ExchangeInstallPath%\FrontEnd\HttpProxy\Ecp. This application runs in the context of an application pool named MSExchangeECPAppPool. In the %ExchangeInstallPath%\FrontEnd\HttpProxy\Ecp directory on your server, you'll find a web.config file that defines the settings for the ECP application.

**FIGURE 6** Viewing the applications that handle Exchange processing.

The Mailbox server where your mailbox resides performs its tasks and processing via the ECP application running on the Exchange Back End website. The physical directory for this application is %ExchangeInstallPath%\ClientAccess\Ecp. This application also runs in the context of an application pool named MSExchangeECPAppPool. In the %ExchangeInstallPath%\ClientAccess\Ecp directory on your server, you'll find a web.config file that defines the settings for the ECP application.

# 3. Getting Started with Exchange Management Shell

Microsoft Exchange Server 2016 includes Exchange Management Shell, which is an extensible command-line environment for Exchange Server that builds on the existing framework provided by Windows PowerShell. When you install Exchange Server 2016 on a server, or when you install the Exchange Server management tools on a workstation, you install Exchange Management Shell as part of the process.

When you start Exchange Management Shell, the working environment is loaded automatically with many of the working environment features coming from profiles, which are a type of script that runs automatically when you start the shell. However, the working environment is also determined by other imported elements.

## Running and Using Cmdlets

A cmdlet (pronounced *commandlet*) is the smallest unit of functionality when working with command shells. You can think of a cmdlet as a built-in command. Rather than being highly complex, most cmdlets are quite simple and have a small set of associated properties.

You use cmdlets the same way you use any other commands and utilities. Cmdlet names are not case sensitive. This means you can use a combination of both uppercase and lowercase characters. After starting the shell, you can type the name of the cmdlet at the prompt, and it will run in much the same way as a command-line command.

For ease of reference, cmdlets are named using verb-noun pairs. The verb tells you what the cmdlet does in general. The noun tells you what specifically the cmdlet works with. For example, the Get-Variable cmdlet gets a named environment variable and returns its value. If you don't specify which variable to get as a parameter, Get-Variable returns a list of all environment variables and their values.

You can work with cmdlets in several ways:

- Executing commands directly at the shell prompt
- Running commands from scripts
- Calling them from C# or other .NET Framework languages

You can enter any command or cmdlet you can run at the shell prompt into a script by copying the related command text to a file and saving the file with the .ps1 extension. You can then run the script in the same way you would any other command or cmdlet. Keep in mind that when you are working with Windows PowerShell, the current directory is not part of the environment path in most instances. Because of this, you typically need to use "./" when you run a script in the current directory, such as:

```
./runtasks
```

> **NOTE** Windows PowerShell includes a rich scripting language and allows the use of standard language constructs for looping, conditional execution, flow control, and variable assignment. Discussion of these features is beyond the scope of this book. A good resource is *Windows PowerShell: The Personal Trainer*.

## Running and Using Other Commands and Utilities

Because the shell runs within the context of the Windows command prompt, you can run all Windows command-line commands, utilities, and graphical applications from within the shell. However, remember that the shell interpreter parses all commands before passing off the command to the command prompt environment. If the shell has a like-named command or a like-named alias for a command, this command, and not the expected Windows command, is executed.

Non–shell commands and programs must reside in a directory that is part of the PATH environment variable. If the item is found in the path, it is run. The PATH variable also controls where the shell looks for applications, utilities, and scripts. In the shell, you can work with Windows environment variables using $env. To view the current settings for the PATH environment variable, type **$env:path**. To add a directory to this variable, use the following syntax:

```
$env:path += ";DirectoryPathToAdd"
```

where *DirectoryPathToAdd* is the directory path you want to add to the path, such as:

```
$env:path += ";C:\Scripts"
```

To have this directory added to the path every time you start the shell, you can add the command line as an entry in your profile. Profiles store frequently used elements, including aliases and functions. Generally speaking, profiles are always loaded when you work with the shell. Keep in mind that cmdlets are like built-in commands rather than standalone executables. Because of this, they are not affected by the PATH environment variable.

## Using Cmdlet Parameters and Errors

You use parameters to control the way cmdlets work. All cmdlet parameters are designated with an initial dash (–). As some parameters are position-sensitive, you sometimes can pass parameters in a specific order without having to specify the parameter name. For example, with Get-Service, you don't have to specify the –Name parameter and can simply type:

```
get-service ServiceName
```

where ServiceName is the name of the service you want to examine, such as:

```
get-service MSExchangeIS
```

Here, the command returns the status of the Microsoft Exchange Information Store service. Because you can use wildcards, such as *, with name values, you can also type get-service mse* to return the status of all Microsoft Exchange–related services.

When you work with cmdlets, you'll encounter two standard types of errors: terminating errors and nonterminating errors. While terminating errors halt execution, nonterminating errors cause error output to be returned but do not halt execution. With either type or error, you'll typically see error text that can help you resolve the problem that caused it. For example, an expected file might be missing or you might not have sufficient permissions to perform a specified task.

## Using Cmdlet Aliases

For ease of use, the shell lets you create aliases for cmdlets. An alias is an abbreviation for a cmdlet that acts as a shortcut for executing the cmdlet. For example, you can use the alias *gsv* instead of the cmdlet name Get-Service.

At the shell prompt, enter **get-alias** to list all currently defined aliases. Define additional aliases using the Set-Alias cmdlet. The syntax is:

```
set-alias aliasName cmdletName
```

where *aliasName* is the alias you want to use and *cmdletName* is the cmdlet for which you are creating an alias. The following example creates a "go" alias for the Get-Process cmdlet:

```
set-alias go get-process
```

To use your custom aliases whenever you work with the shell, enter the related command line in your profile.

# 4. Working with Exchange Management Shell

The Exchange Management Shell is a command-line management interface built on Windows PowerShell. You use the Exchange Management Shell to manage any aspect of an Exchange Server 2016 configuration that you can manage in the Exchange Admin Center. This means that you can typically use either tool to configure Exchange Server 2016. However, only the Exchange Management Shell has the full complement of available commands, and this means that some tasks can be performed only at the shell prompt.

## Starting Exchange Management Shell

After you've installed the Exchange management tools on a computer, the Exchange Management Shell, shown in Figure 7, is available. On desktop computers running Windows 8.1 or Windows 10, one way to start the shell is by using the Apps Search box. Type **shell** in the Apps Search box, and then select Exchange Management Shell. Or click Start, click All Apps and then choose Exchange Management Shell.

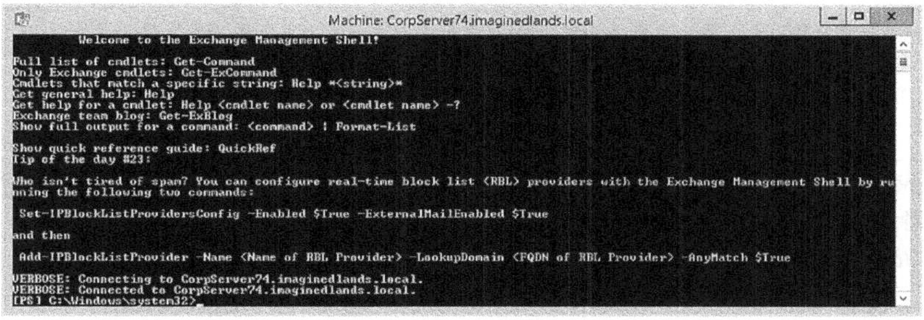

**FIGURE 7** Exchange Management Shell

Starting Exchange Management Shell on Windows Server 2012 R2 or Windows Server 2016 is a little different. Here, click Start and then click the More button to display the Apps screen. On the Apps screen, choose Exchange Management Shell. While you are working with the Apps screen, right-click the tile for Exchange Management Shell and then select Pin To Start or Pin To Taskbar. This will make it easier to access the shell in the future.

Exchange Management Shell is designed to be run only on domain-joined computers. Whether you are logged on locally to an Exchange server or working remotely, starting the shell opens a custom Windows PowerShell console. The console does the following:

1. Connects to the closest Exchange 2016 server using Windows Remote Management (WinRM).

2. Performs authentication checks that validate your access to the Exchange 2016 server and determine the Exchange role groups and roles your account is a member of. You must be a member of at least one management role.

3. Creates a remote session with the Exchange 2016 server. A remote session is a runspace that establishes a common working environment for executing commands on remote computers.

> **NOTE** It's important to note that selecting the shell in this way starts the Exchange Management Shell using your user credentials. This enables you to perform any administrative tasks allowed for your user account and in accordance with the Exchange role groups and management roles you're assigned. As a result, you don't need to run the Exchange Management Shell in administrator mode, but you can. To do so, right-click

Exchange Management Shell shortcut, and then click Run As Administrator.

## Using Exchange Cmdlets

When you are working with the Exchange Management Shell, additional Exchange-specific cmdlets are available. As with Windows PowerShell cmdlets, you can get help information on Exchange cmdlets:

- To view a list of all Exchange cmdlets, enter **get-excommand** at the shell prompt.
- To view a list of Exchange cmdlets for a particular item, such as a user, contact or mailbox, enter **get-help *ItemName***, where *ItemName* is the name of the item you want to examine.

When you work with the Exchange Management Shell, you'll often work with Get, Set, Enable, Disable, New, and Remove cmdlets (the groups of cmdlets that begin with these verbs). These cmdlets all accept the –Identity parameter, which identifies the unique object with which you are working.

Typically, a cmdlet that accepts the –Identity parameter has this parameter as its first parameter, allowing you to specify the identity, with or without the parameter name. When identities have names as well as aliases, you can specify either value as the identity. For example, you can use any of the following techniques to retrieve the mailbox object for the user William Stanek with the mail alias Williams:

```
get-mailbox -identity william
get-mailbox -identity 'William Stanek'
```

```
get-mailbox Williams
get-mailbox "William Stanek"
```

With Get cmdlets, you typically can return an object set containing all related items simply by omitting the identity. For example, if you type **get-mailbox** at the shell prompt without specifying an identity, you get a list of all mailboxes in the enterprise (up to the maximum permitted to return in a single object set).

By default, all cmdlets return data in table format. Because there are often many more columns of data than fit across the screen, you might need to switch to Format-List output to see all of the data. To change to the Format-List output, redirect the output using the pipe symbol (|) to the Format-List cmdlet, as shown in this example:

```
get-mailbox -identity williams | format-list
```

You can abbreviate Format-List as *fl*, as in this example:

```
get-mailbox -identity williams | fl
```

Either technique typically ensures that you see much more information about the object or the result set than if you were retrieving table-formatted data.

## Working with Object Sets and Redirecting Output

When you are working with PowerShell or Exchange Management Shell, you'll often need to redirect the output of one cmdlet and pass it as input to another cmdlet. You can do this using the pipe symbol. For example, if you want to view mailboxes for a specific mailbox database rather than all mailboxes in the enterprise, you can pipe the output of Get-MailboxDatabase to Get-Mailbox, as shown in this example:

```
get-mailboxdatabase –Identity "Engineering" | get-mailbox
```

Here, you use Get-MailboxDatabase to get the mailbox database object for the Engineering database. You then send this object to the Get-Mailbox cmdlet as input, and Get-Mailbox iterates through all the mailboxes in this database. If you don't perform any other manipulation, the mailboxes for this database are listed as output, as shown here:

```
Name               Alias          Server
ProhibitSendQuota
Administrator      Administrator  mailboxsvr82   unlimited
William S          williams       mailboxsvr82   unlimited
Tom G              tomg           mailboxsvr82   unlimited
David W            davidw         mailboxsvr82   unlimited
Kari F             karif          mailboxsvr82   unlimited
Connie V           conniev        mailboxsvr82   unlimited
Mike D             miked          mailboxsvr82   unlimited
```

You can also pipe this output to another cmdlet to perform an action on each individual mailbox in this database. If you don't know the name of the mailbox database you want to work with, enter **get-mailboxdatabase** without any parameters to list all available mailbox databases.

# 5. Working with Exchange Online

Exchange Online is available as part of an Office 365 plan and as a standalone service. Microsoft offers a variety of Office 365 plans that include access to Office Web Apps, the full desktop versions of Office, or both as well as access to Exchange Online. You'll likely want to use an Office 365 midsize business or enterprise plan to ensure Active Directory integration is included as you'll need this feature to create a hybrid Exchange organization. If you don't want to use Office 365, Microsoft offers plans specifically for Exchange Online. The basic plans are the cheapest but don't include in-place hold and data loss prevention features that large enterprises may need to meet compliance and regulatory requirements. That said, both basic and advanced plans support Active Directory integration for synchronization with on-premises Active Directory infrastructure and the creation of hybrid Exchange organizations.

In Exchange Online, email addresses, distribution groups, and other directory resources are stored in the directory database provided by Active Directory for Windows Azure. Windows Azure is Microsoft's cloud-based server operating system. Exchange Online fully supports the Windows security model and by default relies on this security mechanism to control access to directory resources. Because of this, you can control access to mailboxes and membership in distribution groups and perform other security administration tasks through the standard permission set.

Because Exchange Online uses Windows security, you can't create a mailbox without first creating a user account that will use the mailbox. Every Exchange mailbox must be associated with a user account—even those used by Exchange Online for general messaging tasks.

As you get started with Exchange Online, it's important to keep in mind that available features and options can change over time. Why? Microsoft releases cumulative updates for Exchange on a fixed schedule and applies these cumulative updates to their hosted Exchange servers prior to official release of an update for on-premises Exchange servers. Thus, when you see that an update has been released for the current Exchange Server product you know it has been applied to all Exchange Online servers and all of the mailboxes stored in the cloud as well.

## Getting Started with Exchange Online

With Exchange Online, the tools you'll use most often for administration are Office Admin Center and Exchange Admin Center. Regardless of whether you use Exchange Online with Office 365, you'll use Office Admin Center as it's where you manage service-level settings, including the Office tenant domain, subscriptions, and licenses.

## Navigating Exchange Online Services

When you sign up for Exchange Online, you'll be provided an access URL for Office Admin Center, such as https://portal.microsoftonline.com/admin/default.aspx. After you log in by entering your username and password, you'll see the Office Admin Center dashboard, shown in Figure 8.

FIGURE 8  Use Office Admin Center to manage users and accounts

As with Exchange Admin Center, Office Admin Center has a Navigation bar with several options:

**Apps** – Displays a list of the available apps you can switch to, including Office Admin Center.

**Notifications** – Displays notifications, such as alerts regarding licensing or subscription issues.

**Help** – Displays help and feedback options.

**Settings** – Displays options for accessing account settings.

**Account** – Displays the name of the currently logged in user and provides options for accessing the account's profile page and signing out.

Below the Navigation bar, you'll find two buttons:

**Menu** – Displays a menu of options. Click to display the menu. Click again to hide the menu.

**Home** – Displays the Office Admin Center dashboard.

From the Office Admin Center dashboard, you have full access to Office 365 and Exchange Online. Like Office Admin Center, Exchange Admin Center for Exchange Online is a web application. You use Exchange Admin Center for Exchange Online to manage:

- **Organization configuration data.** This type of data is used to manage policies, address lists, and other types of organizational configuration details.

- **Recipient configuration data.** This type of data is associated with mailboxes, mail-enabled contacts, and distribution groups.

Although Exchange Admin Center for on-premises installations and Exchange Admin Center for Exchange Online are used in the same way and have many similarities, they also have many differences. These differences include limitations that apply to the online environment but do not apply to on-premises environments.

The easiest way to access Exchange Admin Center for Exchange Online, shown in Figure 9, is via Office Admin Center:

1. In Office Admin Center, click Menu. If the Admin Centers panel is closed, click it to see the related options.
2. Click Exchange under the Admin Centers heading. This opens the Exchange Admin Center dashboard.

If you are using a mixed or hybrid environment with on-premises and online services, you can also access Office Admin Center and Exchange Admin Center for Exchange Online from your on-premises installation:

1. Access Exchange Admin Center for your on-premises installation and then click Office 365 on the Navigation bar.
2. After your browser connects to Office.com, click Sign In on the Navigation bar and then select Work, School Or University as your account type.

3. Provide the email address and password for your Microsoft account and then click Sign In. This opens Office Admin Center.

4. In Office Admin Center, click Menu and then click Exchange under the Admin Centers heading. This opens the Exchange Admin Center dashboard.

**FIGURE 9** Use the Exchange Admin Center to manage recipients, permissions and more.

The dashboard is unique to Exchange Admin Center for Exchange Online and serves to provide quick access to commonly used features. These features are also available via the Features pane and the related tabs.

Other than the dashboard, Exchange Admin Center for Exchange Online works just like Exchange Admin Center for on-premises installations. Manageable features are listed in the Features pane. After you select a feature in the Features pane, you'll see the related topics or "tabs" for that feature. The manageable items for a selected topic or tab are displayed in the main area of the browser window. For example, when you select Organization in the Features pane, the topics or tabs that you can work with are: Sharing and Apps.

## Understanding Office 365 Licensing

With Exchange Online, you perform administration using either Exchange Admin Center or Windows PowerShell—not Exchange Management Shell, which is meant to be used only with on-premises installations of Exchange. Regardless of which approach you use to create new users in Exchange Online, you must license mailbox users in Office 365. You do this by licensing mailbox plans and associating a mailbox plan with each mailbox user.

Using Exchange Admin Center, you can associate mailbox plans when you create mailbox users or afterward by editing the account properties. In PowerShell, you use the New-Mailbox cmdlet with the –MailboxPlan parameter to do the same.

When you assign mailbox plans, you need to ensure you have enough licenses. You purchase and assign licenses using Office 365 Admin Center:

1. If the Billing options aren't currently displayed in the Features pane, expand Billing by clicking it in the Features pane and then click Licensing to see the number of valid, expired and assigned licenses.

2. Click Subscriptions under Billing in the Features pane to display subscription and licensing options.

3. Click Add Subscriptions to purchase additional services. For example, if you scroll down the list of

purchasable services, you'll see the Exchange Online plans.

4. While viewing plans, click Buy Now to purchase a particular plan. As shown in Figure 10, you'll have the option to specify how many user licenses you want for the selected plan before you check out.

**FIGURE 10** Select a plan and purchase licenses.

Although Office 365 will allow you to assign more mailbox plans than you have licenses for, you shouldn't do this. After the initial grace period, problems will occur. For example, mail data for unlicensed mailboxes may become unavailable. Remember, the number of valid licenses shouldn't exceed the number of assigned licenses.

You activate and license synced users in Office 365 as well. Under Users And Groups > Active Users, select the check boxes for the users you want to activate and license and then select Activate Synced Users. Next, specify the work location for the users, such as United States. Under Assign Licenses, select the mailbox plan to assign. Finally, select Activate.

# 6. Using Windows PowerShell with Exchange Online

Although Office Admin Center and Exchange Admin Center provide everything you need to work with Exchange Online, there may be times when you want to work from the command line, especially if you want to automate tasks with scripts. Enter Windows PowerShell.

## Getting Started with Windows PowerShell

Windows PowerShell is built into Windows and Windows Server. Windows PowerShell supports cmdlets, functions and aliases. Cmdlets are built-in commands. Functions provide basic functionality. Aliases are abbreviations for cmdlet names. As cmdlet, function and alias names are not case sensitive, you can use a combination of both uppercase and lowercase characters to specify cmdlet, function and alias names.

Although Windows PowerShell has a graphical environment called Windows PowerShell ISE (powershell_ise.exe), you'll usually work with the command-line environment. The PowerShell console (powershell.exe) is available as a 32-bit or 64-bit environment for working with PowerShell at the command line. On 32-bit versions of Windows, you'll find the 32-bit executable in the %SystemRoot%\System32\WindowsPowerShell\v1.0 directory.

On 64-bit versions of Windows and Windows Server, a 64-bit and a 32-bit console are available. The default console is the 64-bit console, which is located in the %SystemRoot%\System32\WindowsPowerShell\v1.0 directory.

The 32-bit executable in the
%SystemRoot%\SysWow64\WindowsPowerShell\v1.0
directory and is labeled as Windows PowerShell (x86).

With Windows 8.1 or later, you can start the PowerShell
console by using the Apps Search box. Type **powershell** in
the Apps Search box, and then press Enter. Or you can select
Start and then choose Windows PowerShell. From Mac OS X
or Linux, you can run either Windows 7 or later in a virtual
environment to work with Windows PowerShell.

In Windows, you also can start Windows PowerShell from a
command prompt (cmd.exe) by typing **powershell** and
pressing Enter. To exit Windows PowerShell and return to the
command prompt, type exit.

When the shell starts, you usually will see a message similar to
the following:

```
Windows PowerShell
Copyright (C) 2012 Microsoft Corporation.
All rights reserved.
```

You can disable this message by starting the shell with the –
Nologo parameter, such as:

```
powershell -nologo
```

By default, the version of scripting engine that starts depends
on the operating system you are using. With Windows 8.1 and
Windows Server 2012 R2, the default scripting engine is
version 4.0. With Windows 10 and Windows Server 2016, the
default scripting engine is version 4.0. To confirm the version

of Windows PowerShell installed, enter the following
command:

```
Get-Host | Format-List Version
```

Because you can abbreviate Format-List as FL, you also could
enter:

```
Get-Host | fl Version
```

> **NOTE** Letter case does not matter with Windows
> PowerShell. Thus, Get-Host, GET-HOST and get-host
> are all interpreted the same.

Figure 11 shows the PowerShell window. When you start
PowerShell, you can set the version of the scripting engine
that should be loaded. To do this, use the –Version parameter.
In this example, you specify that you want to use PowerShell
Version 3.0:

```
powershell -version 3
```

> **NOTE** Windows can only load available versions of the
> scripting engine. For example, you won't be able to run
> the version 5.0 scripting engine if only PowerShell
> Version 4.0 is available.

**FIGURE 11** Use the PowerShell console to manage Exchange remotely at the prompt.

By default, the PowerShell window displays 50 lines of text and is 120 characters wide. When additional text is to be displayed in the window or you enter commands and the PowerShell console's window is full, the current text is displayed in the window and prior text is scrolled up. To temporarily pause the display when a command is writing output, press Ctrl+S. You can then press Ctrl+S to resume or Ctrl+C to terminate execution.

## Understanding The Default Working Environment

When you run Windows PowerShell, a default working environment is loaded automatically. The features for this working environment come primarily from profiles, which are a type of script that run automatically whenever you start PowerShell. The working environment also is determined by imported snap-ins, providers, modules, command paths, file associations, and file extensions.

To start Windows PowerShell without loading profiles, use the –Noprofile parameter, such as:

```
powershell -noprofile
```

Whenever you work with scripts, you need to keep in mind the current execution policy and whether signed scripts are required. Execution policy is a built-in security feature of Windows PowerShell that controls whether and how you can run configuration files and scripts. Although the default configuration depends on which operating system and edition are installed, policy is always set on either a per-user or per-computer basis in the Windows registry.

You can display the execution policy currently being applied, using the Get-ExecutionPolicy cmdlet. The available execution policies, from least secure to most secure, are:

- **Bypass.** Bypasses warnings and prompts when scripts run. Use with programs that have their own security model or when a PowerShell script is built into a larger application.
- **Unrestricted.** Allows all configuration files and scripts to run whether they are from local or remote sources and regardless of whether they are signed or unsigned. When you run a configuration file or script from a remote resource, you are prompted with a warning that the file comes from a remote resource before the configuration file is loaded or the script runs.
- **RemoteSigned.** Requires all configuration files and scripts from remote sources to be signed by a trusted publisher. However, configuration files and scripts on the local computer do not need to be signed. PowerShell does not prompt you with a warning before running scripts from trusted publishers.
- **AllSigned.** Requires all configuration files and scripts from all sources—whether local or remote—to be signed by a trusted publisher. Thus, configuration files and scripts on the local computer and remote computers must be signed. PowerShell prompts you with a warning before running scripts from trusted publishers.
- **Restricted.** Prevents PowerShell from loading configuration files and scripts. Effects all configuration files and scripts, regardless of whether they are signed or unsigned. Because a profile is a type of script, profiles are not loaded either.
- **Undefined.** Removes the execution policy that is set for the current user scope and instead applies the execution policy set in Group Policy or for the LocalMachine scope. If

execution policy in all scopes is set to Undefined, the default execution policy, Restricted, is the effective policy.

By default, when you set execution policy, you are using the LocalMachine scope, which is applied to all users of the computer. You also can set the scope to CurrentUser so that the execution policy level is only applied to the currently logged on user.

Using Set-ExecutionPolicy, you can change the preference for the execution policy. Normally, changes to execution policy are written to the registry. However, if the Turn On Script Execution setting in Group Policy is enabled for the computer or user, the user preference is written to the registry, but it is not effective. Windows PowerShell will display a message explaining that there is a conflict. Finally, you cannot use Set-ExecutionPolicy to override a group policy, even if the user preference is more restrictive than the policy setting. For example, you can set the execution policy to run scripts regardless of whether they have a digital signature and work in an unrestricted environment by entering:

```
set-executionpolicy unrestricted
```

When you change execution policy, the change occurs immediately and is applied to the local console or application session. Because the change is written to the registry, the new execution policy normally will be used whenever you work with PowerShell.

## Learning About Cmdlets and Functions

When you are working with Windows PowerShell, you can get a complete list of cmdlets and functions available by entering **get-command**. The output lists cmdlets and functions by name and associated module.

Another way to get information about cmdlets is to use Get-Help. When you enter **get-help \*-\***, you get a list of all cmdlets, including a synopsis that summarizes the purpose of the cmdlet. Rather than listing help information for all commands, you can get help for specific commands by following Get-Help with the name of the cmdlet you want to work with, such as:

```
get-help clear-history
```

Because Windows PowerShell V3 and later use online and updatable help files, you may see only basic syntax for cmdlets and functions when you use Get-Help. To get full help details, you'll have to either use online help or download the help files to your computer. For online help, add the – online parameter to your Get-Help command, such as:

```
get-help get-variable -online
```

You can use the Update-Help cmdlet to download and install the current help files from the Internet. Without parameters, Update-Help updates the help files for all modules installed on the computer. When you are working with Update-Help, keep the following in mind:

- Update-Help downloads files only once a day

- Update-Help only installs files when they are newer than the ones on the computer
- Update-Help limits the total size of uncompressed help files to 1 GB

You can override these restrictions using the –Force parameter.

# 7. Connecting to Exchange Online Using PowerShell

The way you use Windows PowerShell to manage Exchange Server and Exchange Online are different. With Exchange Server installations, you manage Exchange using Exchange Management Shell, which is a command-line management interface built on Windows PowerShell that you can use to manage any aspect of an Exchange Server configuration that you can manage in the Exchange Admin Center. With Exchange Online installations, you manage Exchange using a remote session and the built-in functions and capabilities of Exchange Management Shell are not available.

## Exploring How the Shell Uses Remote Sessions

The Exchange Management Shell is designed to be run only on domain-joined computers and is available when you have installed the Exchange management tools on a management computer or server. Whether you are logged on locally to an Exchange server or working remotely, starting Exchange Management Shell opens a custom Windows PowerShell console that runs in a remote session with an Exchange server.

A remote session is a runspace that establishes a common working environment for executing commands on remote computers. Before creating the remote session, this custom console connects to the closest Exchange server using Windows Remote Management (WinRM) and then performs authentication checks that validate your access to the Exchange server and determine the Exchange role groups and roles your account is a member of. You must be a member of at least one management role.

Because the Exchange Management Shell uses your user credentials, you are able to perform any administrative tasks allowed for your user account and in accordance with the Exchange role groups and management roles you're assigned. You don't need to run the Exchange Management Shell in elevated, administrator mode, but you can by right-clicking Exchange Management Shell, and then selecting Run As Administrator.

By examining the properties of the shortcut that starts the Exchange Management Shell, you can see the actual command that runs when you start the shell is:

```
C:\Windows\System32\WindowsPowerShell\v1.0\powershell.exe -
noexit -command ". 'C:\Program Files\Microsoft\Exchange
Server\V15\bin\RemoteExchange.ps1'; Connect-ExchangeServer -
auto -ClientApplication:ManagementShell "
```

Here, the command starts PowerShell, runs the RemoteExchange.ps1 profile file, and then uses the command Connect-ExchangeServer to establish the remote session. The –Auto parameter tells the cmdlet to automatically discover and try to connect to an appropriate Exchange server. The –ClientApplication parameter specifies that client-side application is the Exchange Management Shell. When you run the shell in this way, Windows Powershell loads a profile script called RemoteExchange.ps1 that sets aliases, initializes Exchange global variables, and loads .NET assemblies for Exchange. The profile script also modifies the standard PowerShell prompt so that it is scoped to the entire Active

Directory forest and defines Exchange-specific functions, including:

- **Get-Exbanner.** Displays the Exchange Management Shell startup banner.
- **Get-Exblog.** Opens Internet Explorer and accesses the Exchange blog.
- **Get-Excommand.** Lists all available Exchange commands.
- **Get-Pscommand.** Lists all available PowerShell commands.
- **Get-Tip.** Displays the tip of the day.
- **Quickref.** Opens Internet Explorer and accesses the Exchange Management Shell quick start guide.

All of these processes simplify the task of establishing an interactive remote session with Exchange server. As implemented in the default configuration, you have a one-to-one, interactive approach for remote management, meaning you establish a session with a specific remote server and work with that specific server whenever you execute commands.

## Establishing Remote Sessions

When you are working with PowerShell outside of Exchange Management Shell, you must manually establish a remote session with Exchange. As the RemoteExchange.ps1 profile file and related scripts are not loaded, the related cmdlets and functions are not available. This means you cannot use Get-Exbanner, Get-Exblog, Get-Excommand, Get-PScommand, Get-Tip or Quickref. Further, when you are working with an online installation of Exchange, the cmdlets available are different from when you are working with Exchange Server.

PowerShell provides several cmdlets for establishing remote sessions, including Enter-PSSession and New-PSSession. The difference between the two options is subtle but important.

## Using an Interactive Remote Session

You can use the Enter-PSSession cmdlet to start an interactive session with Exchange or any other remote computer. The basic syntax is Enter-PSSession ComputerName, where ComputerName is the name of the remote computer, such as the following:

```
enter-pssession Server58
```

When the session is established, the command prompt changes to show that you are connected to the remote computer, as shown in the following example:

```
[Server58]: PS C:\Users\wrstanek.cpand1\Documents>
```

While working in a remote session, any commands you enter run on the remote computer just as if you had typed them directly on the remote computer. Generally, to perform administration, you need to use an elevated, administrator shell and pass credentials along in the session. Establishing a connection in this way uses the standard PowerShell remoting configuration.

However, you cannot connect to Exchange Online using the standard PowerShell remoting configuration. You must go through a PowerShell application running on ps.outlook.com or another appropriate web server. Typically, when you work with Exchange Online, you use the connection URI https://ps.outlook.com/powershell/ and the actual session is redirected to your specific online server. To ensure redirection doesn't fail, you must add the –AllowRedirection parameter.

As shown in the following example, you use the –ConnectionURI parameter to specify the connection URI, the –ConfigurationName parameter to specify the configuration namespace, and the –Authentication parameter to set the authentication type to use:

```
Enter-PSSession -ConfigurationName Microsoft.Exchange
-ConnectionUri https://ps.outlook.com/powershell/
-Authentication Basic -AllowRedirection
```

Here, you set the configuration namespace as Microsoft.Exchange, establish a connection to the Exchange Online URL provided by Microsoft, and use Basic authentication. As you don't specify credentials, you will be prompted to provide credentials.

You also can pass in credentials as shown in this example:

```
Enter-PSSession -ConfigurationName Microsoft.Exchange
-ConnectionUri https://ps.outlook.com/powershell/
-Authentication Basic -Credential
wrstanek@imaginedlands.onmicrosoft.com
-AllowRedirection
```

Here, you pass in credentials and are prompted for the associated password.

Alternatively, you can store credentials in a Credential object and then use Get-Credential to prompt for the required credentials, as shown here:

```
$Cred = Get-Credential
Enter-PSSession -ConfigurationName Microsoft.Exchange
-ConnectionUri https://ps.outlook.com/powershell/
-Authentication Basic -Credential
$Cred -AllowRedirection
```

When you are finished working with Exchange Online, you can end the interactive session by using Exit-PSSession or by typing exit. Although Enter-PSSession provides a quick and easy way to establish a remote session, the session ends when you use Exit-PSSession or exit the PowerShell prompt and there is no way to reestablish the original session. Thus, any commands you are running and any command context is lost when you exit the session.

Thus, as discussed in this section, the basic steps for using a standard interactive remote session are:

1.  Open an administrator Windows PowerShell prompt.
2.  Use Enter-PSSession to establish a remote session.
3.  Work with Exchange Online.
4.  Exit the remote session using Exit-PSSession or by exiting the PowerShell window.

### Creating and Importing A Remote Session

Instead of using a standard interactive session, you may want to create a session that you disconnect and reconnect. To do this, you establish the session using New-PSSession and then import the session using Import-PSSession. The basic syntax:

```
$Session = New-PSSession -ConfigurationName
Microsoft.Exchange -ConnectionUri
https://ps.outlook.com/powershell/
-Authentication Basic -Credential
wrs@imaginedlands.onmicrosoft.com
-AllowRedirection
```

In this example, you use New-PSSession to create a session and store the related object in a variable called $Session. You create the session by setting the configuration namespace as Microsoft.Exchange, establishing a connection to the Exchange Online URL provided by Microsoft, which typically is https://ps.outlook.com, and using HTTPS with Basic authentication for the session. You also allow redirection. Allowing redirection is important as otherwise the session will fail when the Microsoft web servers redirect the session to the actual location of your Exchange Online installation.

To establish the connection, you must always pass in your Exchange Online user name and password. In the previous example, you specify the user name to use and are prompted for the related password. You also could specify the credentials explicitly, as shown here:

```
$Cred = Get-Credential
$Session = New-PSSession -ConfigurationName Microsoft.Exchange
-ConnectionUri https://ps.outlook.com/powershell/
-Authentication Basic -Credential $Cred
-AllowRedirection
```

Here, you store credentials in a Credential object and then use Get-Credential to prompt for the required credentials.

After you establish a session with Exchange Online, you must import the server-side PowerShell session into your client-side session. To do this, you enter the following command:

```
Import-PSSession $Session
```

Where $Session is the name of the variable in which the session object is stored. You can then work with the remote server and Exchange Online.

When you are finished working remotely, you should disconnect the remote shell. It's important to note that, beginning with Windows PowerShell 3.0, sessions are persistent by default. When you disconnect from a session, any command or scripts that are running in the session continue running, and you can later reconnect to the session to pick up where you left off. You also can reconnect to a session if you were disconnected unintentionally, such as by a temporary network outage.

Exchange Online allows each administrative account to have up to three simultaneous connections to sever-side sessions. If you close the PowerShell window without disconnecting from the session, the connection remains open for 15 minutes and then disconnects automatically.

To disconnect a session manually without stopping commands or releasing resources, you can use Disconnect-PSSession, as shown in this example:

```
Disconnect-PSSession $Session
```

Here, the $Session object was instantiated when you created the session and you disconnect while the session continues to be active. As long as you don't exit the PowerShell window in which this object was created, you can use this object to reconnect to the session by entering:

```
Connect-PSSession $Session
```

Later, when you are finished working with Exchange Online, you should remove the session. Removing a session stops any commands or scripts that are running, ends the session, and releases the resources the session was using. You can remove a session by running the following command:

```
Remove-PSSession $Session
```

Thus, as discussed in this section, the basic steps for working with an imported session are:

1. Open an administrator Windows PowerShell prompt.
2. Use New-PSSession to establish the remote session.
3. Import the session using Import-PSSession.
4. Work with Exchange Online. Optionally, disconnect from the session using Disconnect-PSSession and reconnect to the session using Connect-PSSession.
5. Remove the remote session using Remove-PSSession.

# 8. Connecting to Windows Azure

You can manage the Office 365 service, its settings and accounts using either Office Admin Center or Windows PowerShell. Every account you create in the online environment is in fact created in the online framework within which Office 365 and Exchange Online operate. This framework is called Windows Azure, and like Windows Server, it uses directory services provided by Active Directory.

Before you can manage Office 365, its settings, and accounts from Windows PowerShell, you must install the Windows Azure Active Directory module (which is available at the Microsoft Download Center: http://go.microsoft.com/fwlink/p/?linkid=236297). Any computer capable of running Exchange or acting as a management computer can run this module. However, there are several prerequisites, including .NET framework 3.51 and the Microsoft Online Services Sign-in Assistant version 7.0 or later. At the time of this writing, the sign-in assistant was available at http://go.microsoft.com/fwlink/?LinkId=286152. Be sure to download and install only the 64-bit versions of the module and the sign-in assistant.

After you download and install the required components, the Windows Azure Active Directory module is available for your use in any PowerShell window. This module also is referred to as the Microsoft Online module. Although Windows PowerShell 3.0 and later implicitly import modules, you may need to explicitly import this module in some configurations. After you import the module, if necessary, you can connect to the Windows Azure and Microsoft Online Services using the Connect-MSOLService cmdlet.

Because you'll typically want to store your credentials in a Credential object rather than be prompted for them, the complete procedure to connect to Microsoft Online Services by using Windows PowerShell 2.0 is:

```
import-module msonline
$cred = get-credential
connect-msolservice -credential:$cred
```

Or, with Windows PowerShell 3.0 or later, use:

```
$cred = get-credential
connect-msolservice -credential:$cred
```

After connecting to the service, you can use cmdlets for Windows Azure Active Directory to manage online settings and objects. For example, if you want to get a list of user accounts that have been created in the online service along with their licensing status, enter get-msoluser. The results will be similar to the following:

```
UserPrincipalName          DisplayName     isLicensed
-----------------          -----------     ----------
wrstanek@imaginedlands.onm... William Stanek    True
tonyv@imaginedlands.onm...   Tony Vidal        False
```

## Cmdlets for Windows Azure Active Directory

Exchange Online runs on Windows Azure rather than Windows Server. As the two operating environments have different directory services, you must use cmdlets specific to

Active Directory for Windows Azure if you want to work with users, groups and related objects.

You'll find complete information about these cmdlets online at http://msdn.microsoft.com/library/azure/jj151815.aspx. The available cmdlets include:

- **Cmdlets for managing groups and roles**

Add-MsolGroupMember
Add-MsolRoleMember
Get-MsolGroup
Get-MsolGroupMember
Get-MsolRole
Get-MsolRoleMember
Get-MsolUserRole
New-MsolGroup
Redo-MsolProvisionGroup
Remove-MsolGroup
Remove-MsolGroupMember
Remove-MsolRoleMember
Set-MsolGroup

- **Cmdlets for managing licenses and subscriptions**

Get-MsolAccountSku
Get-MsolSubscription
New-MsolLicenseOptions
Set-MsolUserLicense

- **Cmdlets for managing service principals**

Get-MsolServicePrincipal
Get-MsolServicePrincipalCredential
New-MsolServicePrincipal

New-MsolServicePrincipalAddresses
New-MsolServicePrincipalCredential
Remove-MsolServicePrincipal
Remove-MsolServicePrincipalCredential
Set-MsolServicePrincipal

- **Cmdlets for managing users**

Convert-MsolFederatedUser
Get-MsolUser
New-MsolUser
Redo-MsolProvisionUser
Remove-MsolUser
Restore-MsolUser
Set-MsolUser
Set-MsolUserPassword
Set-MsolUserPrincipalName

- **Cmdlets for managing the Azure service**

Add-MsolForeignGroupToRole
Connect-MsolService
Get-MsolCompanyInformation
Get-MsolContact
Get-MsolPartnerContract
Get-MsolPartnerInformation
Redo-MsolProvisionContact
Remove-MsolContact
Set-MsolCompanyContactInformation
Set-MsolCompanySettings
Set-MsolDirSyncEnabled
Set-MsolPartnerInformation

- **Cmdlets for managing domains**

Confirm-MsolDomain

Get-MsolDomain

Get-MsolDomainVerificationDns

Get-MsolPasswordPolicy

New-MsolDomain

Remove-MsolDomain

Set-MsolDomain

Set-MsolDomainAuthentication

Set-MsolPasswordPolicy

- **Cmdlets for managing single sign-on**

Convert-MsolDomainToFederated

Convert-MsolDomainToStandard

Get-MsolDomainFederationSettings

Get-MsolFederationProperty

New-MsolFederatedDomain

Remove-MsolFederatedDomain

Set-MsolADFSContext

Set-MsolDomainFederationSettings

Update-MsolFederatedDomain

You also can enter **get-help *msol*** to get a list of commands specific to Microsoft Online Services.

# 9. Working with Exchange Online Cmdlets

When you work with Exchange Online, the operating environment is different from when you are working with on-premises Exchange Server installations. As a result, different cmdlets and options are available.

## Cmdlets Specific to Exchange Online

Because the operating environment for Exchange Online is different from on-premises Exchange, Exchange Online has cmdlets that aren't available when you are working with on-premises Exchange. You'll find complete information about these cmdlets online at https://technet.microsoft.com/library/jj200780(v=exchg.160).aspx. The additional cmdlets include:

- **Cmdlets for working with online recipients**

Add-RecipientPermission
Get-LinkedUser
Get-RecipientPermission
Get-RemovedMailbox
Get-SendAddress
Import-ContactList
Remove-RecipientPermission
Set-LinkedUser
Undo-SoftDeletedMailbox

- **Cmdlets for working with connected accounts**

Get-ConnectSubscription
Get-HotmailSubscription
Get-ImapSubscription

Get-PopSubscription
Get-Subscription
New-ConnectSubscription
New-HotmailSubscription
New-ImapSubscription
New-PopSubscription
New-Subscription
Remove-ConnectSubscription
Remove-Subscription
Set-ConnectSubscription
Set-HotmailSubscription
Set-ImapSubscription
Set-PopSubscription

- **Cmdlets for working with antispam and anti-malware**

Disable-HostedContentFilterRule
Enable-HostedContentFilterRule
Get-HostedConnectionFilterPolicy
Get-HostedContentFilterPolicy
Get-HostedContentFilterRule
Get-HostedOutboundSpamFilterPolicy
Get-QuarantineMessage
New-HostedConnectionFilterPolicy
New-HostedContentFilterPolicy
New-HostedContentFilterRule
Release-QuarantineMessage
Remove-HostedConnectionFilterPolicy
Remove-HostedContentFilterPolicy
Remove-HostedContentFilterRule
Set-HostedConnectionFilterPolicy
Set-HostedContentFilterPolicy
Set-HostedContentFilterRule

Set-HostedOutboundSpamFilterPolicy

- **Cmdlets for working with connectors**

Get-InboundConnector
Get-OutboundConnector
New-InboundConnector
New-OutboundConnector
Remove-InboundConnector
Remove-OutboundConnector
Set-InboundConnector
Set-OutboundConnector

- **Cmdlets for working with messaging policy and compliance**

Get-DataClassificationConfig
Get-RMSTrustedPublishingDomain
Import-RMSTrustedPublishingDomain
Remove-RMSTrustedPublishingDomain
Set-RMSTrustedPublishingDomain

- **Cmdlets for organization and perimeter control**

Enable-OrganizationCustomization
Get-PerimeterConfig
Set-PerimeterConfig

- **Cmdlets for online reporting**

Get-ConnectionByClientTypeDetailReport
Get-ConnectionByClientTypeReport
Get-CsActiveUserReport
Get-CsAVConferenceTimeReport
Get-CsConferenceReport
Get-CsP2PAVTimeReport
Get-CsP2PSessionReport

Get-GroupActivityReport
Get-MailboxActivityReport
Get-MailboxUsageDetailReport
Get-MailboxUsageReport
Get-MailDetailDlpPolicyReport
Get-MailDetailMalwareReport
Get-MailDetailSpamReport
Get-MailDetailTransportRuleReport
Get-MailFilterListReport
Get-MailTrafficPolicyReport
Get-MailTrafficReport
Get-MailTrafficSummaryReport
Get-MailTrafficTopReport
Get-MessageTrace
Get-MessageTraceDetail
Get-MxRecordReport
Get-OutboundConnectorReport
Get-RecipientStatisticsReport
Get-ServiceDeliveryReport
Get-StaleMailboxDetailReport
Get-StaleMailboxReport

Although cmdlets specific to Windows Azure Active Directory and Exchange Online itself are available, many of the cmdlets associated with on-premises Exchange continue to be available as well. Primarily, these cmdlets include those that are specific to recipients and mailboxes and do not include those specific to Exchange on-premises configurations or to Exchange server configurations. For example, you can continue to use cmdlets for working with mailboxes, including Disable-Mailbox, Enable-Mailbox, Get-Mailbox, New-Mailbox, Remove-Mailbox, and Set-Mailbox. However, you cannot use cmdlets for working with mailbox databases. In Exchange Online, mailbox databases are managed automatically as part of the service.

## Working with Exchange Online Cmdlets

When you work with the Exchange Online, you'll often use Get, Set, Enable, Disable, New, and Remove cmdlets. The groups of cmdlets that begin with these verbs all accept the – Identity parameter, which identifies the unique object with which you are working. Generally, these cmdlets have the – Identity parameter as the first parameter, which allows you to specify the identity, with or without the parameter name.

For identities that have names as well as aliases, you can specify either value as the identity. For example, to retrieve the mailbox object for the user William Stanek with the mail alias Williams, you can use any of the following techniques:

```
get-mailbox Williams
get-mailbox -identity williams
get-mailbox "William Stanek"
get-mailbox -identity 'William Stanek'
```

Typically, Get cmdlets return an object set containing all related items when you omit the identity. For example, if you enter get-mailbox without specifying an identity, PowerShell displays a list of all mailboxes available (up to the maximum permitted to return in a single object set).

Cmdlets can display output is several different formats. Although all cmdlets return data in table format by default, there are often many more columns of data than fit across the screen. For this reason, you might need to output data in list format.

To output in list format, redirect the output using the pipe symbol (|) to the Format-List cmdlet, as shown in this example:

```
get-mailbox "William Stanek" | format-list
```

Because fl is an alias for Format-List, you also can use fl, as in this example:

```
get-mailbox "William Stanek" | fl
```

With a list format output, you should see much more information about the object or the result set than if you were retrieving table-formatted data.

Note also the pipe symbol (|) used in the examples. When you are working with Windows PowerShell, you'll often need to use the pipe symbol (|) to redirect the output of one cmdlet and pass it as input to another cmdlet. For example, access to remote PowerShell is a privilege for an online user that can be viewed with Get-User and managed with Set-User. To determine whether a particular user has remote shell access, you can enter:

```
Get-User UserID | fl RemotePowerShellEnabled
```

where UserID is the identity of the user to view, such as:

```
Get-User WilliamS | fl RemotePowerShellEnabled
```

If the user should have remote PowerShell access but doesn't currently, you can enable access using the –

RemotePowerShellEnabled parameter of Set-User, as shown in this example:

```
Set-User WilliamS -RemotePowerShellEnabled $true
```

If the user has remote PowerShell access but shouldn't, you can disable access byh setting the –RemotePowerShellEnabled to $false, as shown in this example:

```
Set-User TonyG -RemotePowerShellEnabled $false
```

When you work with list- or table-formatted data, you may want to specify the exact data to display. For example, with Get-User, you can display only the user name, display name and remote PowerShell status using:

```
Get-User | Format-Table Name, DisplayName,
RemotePowerShellEnabled
```

If your organization has a lot of users you can prevent the result set from getting truncated by allowing an unlimited result set to be returned, as shown in this example:

```
Get-User -ResultSize Unlimited | Format-Table
Name,DisplayName,RemotePowerShellEnabled
```

With cmdlets that have many properties, you may want to filter the output based on a specific property. For example, to display a list of all users who have remote PowerShell access, you can filter the result set on the RemotePowerShellEnabled property, as shown in the following example:

```
Get-User -ResultSize unlimited -Filter
{RemotePowerShellEnabled -eq $true}
```

Alternatively, you may want to see a list of users who don't have remote PowerShell access. To do this, filter the results by looking for users who have the RemotePowerShellEnabled property set to $False:

```
Get-User -ResultSize unlimited -Filter
{RemotePowerShellEnabled -eq $false}
```

Thank you for purchasing *Presenting Exchange*!

Find more books by William Stanek online at your favorite store.

Stanek &
Associates

# THE PERSONAL TRAINER™

## Windows 10

## William Stanek
Award-winning technology expert

# Index

www.ingramcontent.com/pod-product-compliance
Lightning Source LLC
Chambersburg PA
CBHW061033050326
40689CB00012B/2803